Gallery Books
*Editor*: Peter Fallon
O RATHAILLE

Michael Hartnett

# O RATHAILLE

Gallery Books

*O Rathaille*
is first published
simultaneously in paperback
and in a clothbound edition
in December 1998.

The Gallery Press
Loughcrew
Oldcastle
County Meath
Ireland

*All rights reserved. For permission
to reprint or broadcast these poems
write to The Gallery Press.*

© Michael Hartnett 1998

ISBN 1 85235 209 4 (*paperback*)
     1 85235 210 8 (*clothbound*)

The Gallery Press acknowledges the financial assistance
of An Chomhairle Ealaíon / The Arts Council, Ireland,
and the Arts Council of Northern Ireland.

# Contents

Introduction *page* 11
The Translation 13

VISION POEMS
  The Dream 14
  The Merchant's Son 15
  Silver of Silver 17

ELEGIES
  Elegy on Father John Mac Inery 20
  On the Death of Tadhg Ó Cróinín's Three Children 23
  On the Death of Gerald, Son of the Knight of Glin 25

OCCASIONAL POEMS
  Death: a Dialogue 33
  The Geraldines' Daughter 34
  On a Cock Stolen from a Good Priest 36
  On a Gift of Shoes 38

POLITICAL POEMS
  The Wounds of Ireland 43
  The Ruin that Befell the Great Families of Ireland 45
  The Prophecy of Don Fírinne 48

SATIRICAL POEMS
  On the Death of Murty Griffin 50
  Domhnall na Tuille's Satire on Ó Rathaille 52
  Ó Rathaille's Answer 55

THE BIG HOUSE
  The Poet at Castle Tochar 59
  Excerpts 60

THE BROWNS
  Elegy for John Brown  64
  The Good Omen  68
  Epithalamium for Lord Kenmare  69
  Valentine Brown  71

DESTITUTION
  The Time He Moved beside Tonn Tóime  74
  The Poet on His Death-bed  75

*Acknowledgements  78*

*for Reverend Pádraig Ó Fiannachta, P.P.*
*Canon of Dingle*

## Introduction

Tradition says that Aodhagán Ó Rathaille was born at *Screathan an Mhíl* (Scrahanaveal) in County Kerry, c.1670, some ten miles east of Killarney and six miles to the south-east of Scartaglin. When Ó Rathaille was a child his father died and left his mother in possession of half the townland of Scrahanaveal; but times got hard and the family moved to *Cnoc an Chorrfhia* (Stagmount), seven miles south-east of *Na Mínteoga* (Meentogues) in Kilcummin (where Eoghan Rua Ó Súilleabháin was born in 1748, some twenty years after the death of Ó Rathaille). Ó Rathaille lived there for some years; there is (or was) a well in Stagmount called Aodhagán's Well. Perhaps he lived later in Lisaby and Killarney, but he *did* live near Castlemaine (see 'The Time He Moved beside Tonn Tóime, p. 74). He was in Dromcollogher, County Limerick, in 1722; Dáibhí Ó Bruadair had died in that area in 1698. There he made a copy of Keating's *Forus Feasa ar Éirinn*. This manuscript is in the National Library of Ireland. It is inscribed 'Ar na scríobh le hAodhagán Ua Raghaillaigh do Ruighri mic Seáin oig mhic Sithe a n-Drom Coluchair 'san m-bliadhain d'aois Chriosd mile seacht (gcéad) agus an dara bliadhain fithchead. July an seachtmhadh lá.' (Written by Aodhagán Ó Rathaille for Rory son of Seán Óg Mac Sheehy in Dromcollogher in the year of the age of Christ, 1722. July the seventh day.) The MS is signed at the end *Finis liber secondi 7br the 9th 1722*. Aodhagán Ua Rathaille. (End of the second book, September the 9th 1722.) The poet varies the signature of his surname on occasion; as he is now more widely known as Ó Rathaille, that is the form I shall use in this book. He died sometime after 1727 and is possibly buried in Muckross Abbey, Killarney.

## The Translation

I have written elsewhere to the effect that Frank O'Connor was *the* voice of Ó Rathaille for my generation. Nevertheless I began translating this work in 1993 to give the reader a fuller view of the work of this great poet.

My approach to the translating of the poetry of the 17th and 18th centuries has changed somewhat; now it is looser, the rhymes more slack, but I have, to the best of my ability, maintained the metres and rhythm.

*Vision Poems*

## *The Dream*

One dawn, before Titan had thought of stirring his feet,
I had climbed to a hill-top, pleasant and steep;
flocks of maidens I met, from misery free,
a muster that lived in a white house of the Sí.

A magical haze they'd arranged where no darkness appeared,
from Galway of bright-coloured stones to Cork of the quays;
nut-clusters and fruit grew forever on trees,
acorns eternal in woods and honey on stones could be seen.

Three candles they lit, with a light I cannot describe,
in Connello the red, high on Knockfierna's side;
to Thomond I followed, this hooded flock as my guide,
and I asked: 'In your rounds what secret hides in this rite?'

Aoibhill, in whom no darkness appeared,
when asked, 'Why light three candles in all of the quays?'
said, 'In the name of the king that we'll soon see,
guarding three kingdoms through eternity.'

I started quite suddenly out of my dream;
all the joy Aoibhill mentioned was true — so it seemed.
But truly I trembled; unhappy, afraid, ill at ease,
one dawn, before Titan had thought of stirring his feet.

# The Merchant's Son

A vision clear I saw myself, in bed and I exhausted:
a gentle girl, whose name was Éire, approaching me on
   horseback.
With full green eyes and hair thick-curled, bright slim waist
   and eyebrows,
she did proclaim, that on the way, with zeal, was Mac an
   Cheannaí.

Her mouth so sweet, her voice so meek (beloved by us that
   girl is),
the wife of Brian whom soldiers served — my utter ruin her
   anguish.
By foreign flails so beaten down, my slender fair-haired
   cousin,
there's no relief to come near her till back comes Mac an
   Cheannaí.

Hundreds there are in pain that pine for her lovely body
(offspring of kings, Míleadh's sons, dragons fierce in action);
her face is sad, she does not stir; though grieving and
   enfeebled,
there's no relief to come near her till back comes Mac an
   Cheannaí.

She said herself — her story's sad and my total ruin her
   heartache —
she'd no music now, she weeps aloud, though her troops
   unfalse were gallant;
her clergy's gone, she's in great pain, a leftover for all
   mongrels;
she'll barren become and lie with none till back comes Mac
   an Cheannaí.

And she said again, this tender girl, that since all her kings
    were conquered,
Conn and Art who fiercely reigned with plunder-hand in
    battle,
Criomhthan the strong who brought hostages home and
    Laoiseach Mac Chéin the mighty,
she'll barren become and lie with none till back comes Mac
    an Cheannaí.

She looks to the south every other day, to the beach of the
    ships, poor creature;
she looks to the east and stares at the sea — my grief tonight
    her anguish;
she looks to the west with hope in her God, over slanting
    sand-shot breakers —
she'll barren become and lie with none till back comes Mac
    an Cheannaí.

Her freckled kin, they're overseas, the crowds who loved
    this woman;
no favour, feast, can be had by them, no fondness, love, I
    witness;
her face is wet, no sleep she gets — black with gloom her
    aspect —
there's no relief to come near her till back comes Mac an
    Cheannaí.

I said to her when I heard her words, 'The love you knew
    was mortal,
beyond in Spain his body's laid and none will heed your
    heartache.'
When she heard my voice so close beside, her body shook
    with screaming,
her soul escaped in one quick flash: my woe, this girl,
    exhausted.

## Silver of Silver

Silver of silver I saw on a path so lonely;
crystal of crystal, the blue of her eyes tinged greenly;
sweetness of sweetness, her phrases not gloomy with
   ageing;
redness and whiteness all mixed in her cheeks — they
   were glowing.

Plaiting on plaiting in each rib of her golden ringlets,
stealing the shining from earth with their long sweeping;
ornaments clearer than glass on her breasts so buoyant,
whose origins were in the sky where she was created.

Much news with knowledge she told me, being lonely,
news of him to return to his land by right of royalty;
news of the fall of the gangs who caused his expulsion
and more news that I'll not put in my song — for I fear
   it.

Folly of follies, I came up close beside her,
caught by the captive who tied me up so tightly;
I called Mary's Son for help and she sprang away from
   me;
that woman flashed off to the spirits' house in Sliabh
   Luachra.

I ran with mad speed, I sped with heart pounding,
through edges of swamps, through marsh and red level
   moorland;
to the strong house I came (I do not know by what path-
   way),
to that dwelling of dwellings, built by magic of druids.

They scoffed at me mockingly, this crowd of goblins,
young women whispered and tossed their long-curled
   hair at me;

in shackles and fetters they bound me uncomfortably,
while my girl, breast to breast, with a stout, loutish
   fellow lay.

I said to her then, in severest of sentences,     25
how ill it became her to unite with that churlish one
while a thrice-fairer man of the Gaelic race awaited her,
awaited her still, to be a sweet bride to him.

Hearing my voice she cried out — her pride was so
   wounded;     29
streams of tears flowed down her red cheeks so freely,
and she sent me a guide to guard me out of the ghost-
   house,
silver of silver I met on a path so lonely.

The sorrow, the pang, the tragic loss, the grief!     33
The bright, belovèd one, tender, warm-lipped and sweet,
held by a balding, jaundiced lecher and his black team;
there's no relief for her till the lions come over the sea.

*Elegies*

## Elegy on Father John Mac Inery

The kind, pious priest's departed,
servant of Pan, good at almsgiving;
a great light of superb qualities,
a star of knowledge, a Paul in his sayings.

Withered, the lovely perfumed apple;
withered, the tree and the plant in flower;
the gentle vine, fair and sympathetic,
the branch of palm from lovely Paradise.

Withered, the tongue not bitter in talking,
the messenger who came from Heaven;
the servant, cordial and generous,
who protected sinners from Satan.

Mercury's withered, a tower against foemen,
a hunting hound, who championed merriment,
the people's torch without corruption or cunning
and a plough-ox who did not cheat his master.

The kind and welcoming huntsman's left us;
he followed the track and life of St Patrick;
a routing Oscar, noble and daring,
who overthrew the self-conceited.

This Goll died who was strong and clever,
who sent greed down a cliff with its partners;
the psalm-singer died, the student of David,
who did not think of Lust or Envy.

He did not love Gluttony, the man I speak of;
till he died he controlled the body's evil;
he hated Anger and took no part in it;
he routed Sloth down the pathway headlong.

He was a lovely strong-hearted hero,           29
seven times better than Ajax in battle;
thrice better at the sword than that chieftain,
great Alexander of Macedonia.

Mary's spouse, though she is also his mother,     33
dear son of Christ, through his love for Him;
keeper of Paradise, battle-gauntlet,
God's captain or one of his guardsmen.

The ill and sinning soul's physician,            37
Christ's physician, for His white sheep-flock;
the Father's physician, for the impious sinner,
physician to the sick, the injured, the tormented.

Sweet timbrel for the songs of David,          41
the lovely harp of the hall of angels;
physician who healed those wounded by Satan,
Mary's servant, her gun in the battle-breach.

Physician for the ravenous, naked, hungry,     45
physician of the blind in their time of danger;
physician of the weak, their protecting banner,
physician of women, men, and infants.

Master of a ship that lacked no cable          49
in the false sea of this drowned existence;
the spoiler of Acheron, beloved by the weakling,
he bound the demons in a desert.

A calm and wise man like Solomon,            53
vigorous, courteous, giving, providing;
placid, pleasant, benign in his temperament,
well-known, spirited, polite and calm-faced.

Prudent, moderate, chaste and smiling, 57
not seen in him were pride and vanity;
just, holy, giver of alms from the blood-line
of the O'Briens, strong, masterful and stalwart.

Pure he came from the house of Kincora, 61
from the true kings of the land of Fáilbhe;
from the race of Lachtna, of Cas of great plunder;
overseas they scattered the horde from Denmark.

The congregation's sad at his going, 65
the air is troubled at his departing,
the water reddens . . .

# On the Death of Tadhg Ó Cróinín's Three Children

Rathmore gave a scream; shattered her looms,
her fortune was ruined. Sorrow's house did explode,
a total fog fell. I could not see the lawn.
To that lime-white place tears came with the news.

Destroyed by great force by the strongest of floods
her delft and her jewels, her wicker, her songs;
a swift spark jumped up to her forehead, that burned
her smooth richest quilts, her goblets of gold.

Gloom hurting and pangs that wound without cure;
great loss in the West, and a fever so black
caused a longing to weep, a heavy heart-spasm;
Eilín in the grave, and Diarmuid, and Tadhg.

Oh God, who did die, whom the blind man did wound,
to your holy house convey the trapped three;
grant richness of sense to their father, I pray,
so he can bow down before your sacred will.

Three perfect pearls, well-trained in their ways,
three sun-bright candles, three clever in deeds;
three corn-ears unbowed, and not old in years,
three stars without pride in words or in traits;

   three strings that were sweet (three holes in the
      ground),
three saintly children who gave great love to Christ;
three mouths and three hearts, three fine bodies in
      graves,
three foreheads so bright where black beetles parade.

Three vines that were fair, three true doves so wise,  25
three apples so fine from a fresh royal branch;
these stewards of the house used no thrift to the poor,
three smooth faces, slim waists; they darken my heart.

Their loss, it triples my loss and triples my grief,  29
the three mild and saintly, the perfume-skinned three,
since the grave snatched away my three most refined,
oh King, direct them to your mansion most royal.

# On the Death of Gerald, Son of the Knight of Glin

For whom are our chieftains dressed in mourning?  1
Who caused the face of the sun to be wounded?
Who, but a prince of Grecian root-stock,
shut without life beneath a tombstone.

Hawk of Munster, hero of valour,  5
hawk of Glin and son of kindness;
hawk of Shannon, powerful Oscar,
hawk much loved in Féidhlim's island.

Phoenix, smooth-limbed and great-hearted,  9
phoenix of trophies, wisdom his trademark;
phoenix of the Liffey and Lithe, my sorrow!
phoenix, nimble, who guarded us bravely.

Pearl of fertile Castlemartyr,  13
pearl of Cloyne, calm-faced and shining;
pearl of the Suir, pride of the Irish,
pearl of Limerick, quick trout of the Féile.

Overlord, pious, shrewd, accomplished  17
overlord, law-maker, learnèd, fearless;
overlord of the slim blue sword-blades,
overlord of action in strong Banba.

Ear of wheat, without weeds or bending,  21
heart of mail, head of his kinsmen;
suit of armour, for all unbroken,
shelter from torment, grief and danger.

Candle of knowledge, rose of Ireland,　　　　　　　　25
candle of knowledge, torch of princes;
sun of bright daylight, waxen taper,
blood of strength and famous taper.

Vinetree, lovely, flower of soldiers,　　　　　　　　29
vinetree of the sons of valour;
vinetree, leader of jewelled Connello,
vinetree of Callan, scion of heroes.

Rose unwithered till withered by dying,　　　　　　33
rose of the lions, comet of Heaven;
rose of kings most exalted in Ireland,
rose of the poets, shelter of clerics.

Summoner of all West Limerick,　　　　　　　　　37
summoner of Glin (oh his wounded comrades!);
summoner of Dingle — I make no lies up —
summoner, defender with his soldiers.

Gearalt Mac Thomáis, lover of ladies,　　　　　　　41
torrent of the springtide with its breakers;
one fit to rule three kingdoms taken —
his life's thread Atropos has broken.

The grief, the woe, the thousand woundings,　　　　45
the agony, the pain caused by this man's dying;
sorrow returns and tears come with it —
Gearalt under stones, subdued and lifeless.

Here lies a Norman-Irish sapling,　　　　　　　　　49
a head of curls, not morose, not impulsive,
a head of understanding in judgement,
a head where none saw misery of feature.

His eyes were blue as the sky is azure,
his tongue was sweet, courteous in speaking;
complete and perfect his fine teeth were,
his eyebrows slender, proper, narrow.

His hands when armed were hard to conquer,
hands of exploits, well of humanity;
his waist, a lion's in heroic struggle;
his heart was big, his voice stentorian.

Because he had died they came quickly,
the four elements, roaring in chorus;
showers of blood poured down in vehemence
and banshees were in torment in all districts —

in Kenry, his own, fine, rightful holding,
wringing her tears was lovely Cíobán,
and Úna, Aoife, Déirdre and Clíodhna;
and in Sídh Beidhbhe, Maedhbh bitterly weeping;

in Sídh Cruachna a flood from the heavens,
in Sídh Bainne by the Flesk, and on the Claodach;
in Sídh Tuirc by the Laune's edges,
in Sídh Beidhbh of the ancient brooches.

A woman admitted his right to Claonghlais,
the women of Cooney were tortured by sorrow;
in Timoleague the women were screaming,
in Imokilly and on the Deele-side.

A woman admitted his right (and his kinsmens')
in Youghal and the rich land of the Roches,
in Tralee and beside Loch Éirne,
beside Casán and in Kinalmeaky.

On hearing the news about the Phoenix 81
Tonn Clíodhna gave a dangerous spasm,
Lough Gur for seven days was bloody
and the Maine was two months dry though crying.

The Lithe locked up her free-flowing waters, 85
the sun's complexion turned coal-black;
mast stayed on no oak nor osier.
Ireland deserted her friend and husband.

The havens of Heavens flushed quite scarlet, 89
in the sky the stars sank downwards;
the shapes of birds became disfigured.
Human creation was extinguished.

Nothing's prepared on the bare hill-pastures, 93
no crops on limestone land or tillage;
in the beaks of birds there is no music,
the flower-bright harp of Ireland is silent.

Gearalt was a friend to all the clergy, 97
a swift Goll Mac Mórna, in battle unconquered;
a Cúchulainn, for astonishing actions,
a Conall Gulban, an Oscar for fighting.

He was the tower that gave hope to Ireland, 101
*she* gave him love and her heart's affection;
she gave him friendship and care above hundreds,
she announced delight in his love and their union;

Little wonder that she did this — 105
for there was no blood of the kings of Ireland,
north or south, throughout this island,
that was not strained through his entire system.

On hearing of his fate, this woman 109
was greatly startled and astonished,
and she swore, as she grew in greyness,
never again to lie with a husband.

Many chieftains were loved by the harlot — 113
they gained her hand, her bed, her chattels;
they gained her desires, her consent, her loving;
they fell, defending her, into captivity.

His going so young to decay is my torture, 117
in the family grave of his noble ancestors,
stretched in a tomb, in a trench, in a rock-cave
beside the heroes of the free-born Geraldines.

When this warrior was baptised as an infant — 121
vine of the Kingdom of Conn, of the hundred battles —
he got love from the heart of Mercury
who pressed much honey into his fingers.

Mars in his childhood made him a hero, 125
gave him a bright blue sword and armour
and a smooth helmet to protect him in trouble,
a breastplate also and command over soldiers.

He got wisdom from the god of Wisdom, 129
intellect, memory, common sense, refinement;
mind and knowledge, liveliness and learning,
kindness, tranquility and beauty.

He got from Pan every gift possible: 133
a stanchion to herd five provinces,
wax in plenty to heal his sheepflocks
and dogs to guard them from the wolfpacks.

He got a clear smooth skin from Venus
and a voracious forge from Vulcan;
Neptune gave him a ship for the open ocean
and Oceanus a pumping engine.

My heart's great woe, my thousand torments,
the Glen of the Knight sheds tears in torrents —
no starling's music, no sweet birds call there —
its luck, its good, its star has fallen.

His death took from her Ireland's laughter —
now beetle-black are her bright colours;
her nostrils and her eyes are rheumy,
the marrow from her bones is oozing.

I ask for the soul of the sword-shattering falcon,
whose death brought gloom on our liberal mansions,
eternal glory without loss or danger
above in sunlight, intimate with Heaven;

who from Shannon to Beare left a stain not erasable,
who coloured all black the splendid sunshine,
who left the land of Fál all tearful
from Carn in the south to northern Aileach.

Lily among thorns, yew without bent branches,
gold of champions, champion of warriors;
of a royal flock, most noble in Ireland,
who never felt fear in fight or in danger.

Leath Mhogha regarded him with envy
because his good surpassed the gentry's;
as the choicest flowers are scattered
his fame and manners spread unclouded.

Bright son of the Knight of noble-shipped Shannon, 165
envy of all men, blood of free princes;
a heart not cold that everyone cherished,
a benefactor to the weak of Ireland.

Brave was his brow in times of trouble, 169
bright was his heart, his breast, his senses,
his mind without malice, his mettle was likewise —
in all these traits no contempt or weakness.

*The Epitaph*

Oh tall death-stone, beneath you lies, demeaned, 173
the poor man's friend, the strong shoot fresh and clean,
defender of lovers, of royal blood and gentle shape —
Gearald of Glin (the bitterness!) lies beneath your
  weight.

Beneath your weight lies lifeless, Gearalt the Grecian; 177
royal prince and seer, who excelled all chieftains;
till his life was over, a faultless man, and learnèd —
may Christ take him without delay to holy Heaven.

*(c.1709)*

*Occasional Poems*

## Death: a Dialogue

*Aodhagán was asked by a priest to compose a poem that contained no lies.*

A: Great George will die, who is High King over us,
and George from the banks of the Maigue will follow him;
Mór will die and her children will be sorrowful.
And John Bowen and Kate Stephen? Death will swallow them.

P: Hold on, my poet, and don't be so hasty;
don't give snap judgements on good reputations;
though many learnèd men have met their downfall
it's not right to conclude that 'twas Death that caused it.

A: The horse will die though long and lithe his stride;
hen, duck, and hawk and dove — they will not survive;
fame and family, woman, man and child,
and that snug and greedy priest: all of them will die.

P: Honest Aodhagán, now — answer us out straight.
Since young children and old women will share the same fate —
where will they go? Will *they* see God's glory
or suffer pain forever, Kate Stephen and John Bowen?

A: The crowd who practise boozing, drinking lots of wine,
and stuff themselves with meat on Friday when they dine,
if it's glory that they'll get in reward for such a feat,
then John Bowen and Kate Stephen need have no fear.

(c.1704)

## The Geraldines' Daughter

Oh pearl that is cloudless, you tempt me, don't doubt it;
   don't be angry, hear me out and I'll tell you my tale;
you showered shafts and darts that came sharply at me,
   to my wounded heart, and I aimless became.
To tell the truth, I'd rather go to Egypt from the harbour
   and to Ireland, willingly, I'd not come back;
but on strong seas or in meadows, in happiness, in fetters,
   I'd not grieve if I were near you, poor on a riverbank.

Flowing down and plaited, in waves and in thick clusters,
   are your gold tresses, shining with grace;
your pearl-eyes adorn you, like stars of the morning,
   and eyebrows, as if by pen-strokes, slenderly shaped.
So lovely to look upon, cheeks, lime-white like snow is,
   gaily contend with the rose-richness in your face;
they brought Phoebus hastening to see *you* above all maidens,
   his forehead was on fire with desire for your shape.

Pure white your breasts are, like swans about a jetty,
   your snow-white, small body like a seagull in hue;
all of your goodness can't be put on parchment,
   a gentle, mild lily, the pick of all girls, are you.
Your lips, they are crimson, your white teeth are blemishless,
   they would keep all disease from thousands like me;
your tongue's noble speech, schooled in the histories
   brought stags from the mountain-peaks, the sound was so sweet.

A Phoenix of the Geraldines, the Grecians of the harbour,
   mild sister to Clanna Míleadh of the battle-bands;
heroes, without mercy, subdued by the English,
   have no wealth or mansion, have no strength or land.

It's no lie the blood of Powers and the blood of Barrys  29
   of the strong hounds of Bunratty is filtered through
     you twice;
there's no free prince or dragon of the race of Cashel,
   who's not related to you, girl, immaculate and mild.

I do not know the likes of her, in England or Ireland,  33
   for achievement, personality, intellect and form,
this clever girl's better far it is reported
   than Helen for whom thousands died in a war.
There's no man alive who'd see her in the morning,  37
   see her cheerful face, whose grief would not fade;
my bondage and my hardship! I can't avoid her presence
   in my sleeping, in my dreaming, by night or by day.

## On a Cock Stolen from a Good Priest

*Whereas* Aongus, wise in prophecy,
   a pious priest and Christian man;
today into my presence came
   complaining, stating truthfully

that he bought a cock of pedigree
   for his street-hens and his household-hens
of lovely crow, and beautiful,
   and his nape was gleaming, colour-full;

that he gave fifty shillings for
   a bird speckle-backed delightfully,
till a changeling with powers magical
   stole it from the market-place.

A man like him most certainly
   needs a crowing cock to wake him up,
to watch in case of dozing off
   every time that Vespers call.

Because of this, I order ye,
   ye state-bailiffs of this court of mine,
let ye search all the highways out
   and that with zeal and earnestness;

leave no *lios* or fairy-hill
   where ye hear noise or rattling sounds
without chasing the cross fairy-thing
   that did this deed of plundering.

*Wheresoever* in what hiding-place
   ye find this heavy pot-belly,
bring him here in cords tied up
   that I may hang him for the wretch he is.

For your so doing as your duty 'tis
   you now by me are authorised.
Written by my hand and quill
   in this era of the President.

## On a Gift of Shoes

I received jewels of outstanding beauty —
two shoes, supple and finished smoothly;
they came from the south — Barbary leather
brought by the fleet of King Philip hither;

two shoes decorated with neat trimming,
two shoes that will last while tramping hill-tops,
two shoes of well-cut, well-tanned leather,
two shoes that protect me in rough meadows;

two shoes noble, and they're not tight-fitting,
two shoes stalwart, when hurting foe-men,
two shoes narrow, without split or wrinkle,
two shoes well-made, without seam or opening;

two shoes, hardy and brave in high places,
of the hide torn from the white cow's carcass —
the cow that was guarded in the waste-land
and tended with care by a giant watchman.

And a god, he loved her for a season
and saddened and darkened her brother's reason;
till one night she was stolen by a bailiff
from the hundred-eyed head, that ugly doomed creature.

Shoes from her hide the rain cannot soften
nor can heat harden their soles and uppers;
the wind can't destroy their lovely lustre
nor too much heat make them shrink or shrivel.

The soles and uppers were bound with bristles,
feather-like, lovely, belonging to Túis,
brought in a ship by the children of Tuireann
to Lugh the vigorous, the mighty.

Better shoes poets never dreamed of         29
nor did Achilles get their like for comfort
in his legacy — which brought grief to Ajax;
he did not get them, for all his declaiming.

The awl that pierced the hide I tell ye of         33
was made of the hardest steel that ever was;
for seven hundred years the demons were
making its spike with Vulcan's connivance.

Black hemp grew on the rim of Acheron         37
and was spun by hags, companions of Atropos;
by this was sewn my fine shoes' edges,
by the magic power of the Fates most potent.

They were once designed for Darius         41
till Alexander overcame him;
they were for a time on mighty Caesar
till from his feet were robbed the world's playthings.

They were owned for a time by the gods of Fáilbhe,         45
by famous Lir, and the plunderer, Lughaidh;
by Bodhbh Dearg, once our supporter,
by battering Balar who throve in slaughter.

Long time in Magh Seanaibh's fairy mansion,         49
and Aoibheall had them and men of ancient magic;
they do not wear out, or lose their appearance —
from a man of welcomes I received them.

Kind Domhnall, Cathal's son — now, hear me —         53
he's a luck-bringing chieftain and true hero
of the seed of Glenflesk who knelt to no man,
he presented these shoes to me as a token.

They cure all pain, all problems and all illness,   57
hoarseness, frenzy, falling sickness;
thirst, starvation, biting hunger,
torment, torture; the stress of going under.

Against enemies, in war and conflict,   61
with these each breach was charged by Oscar;
though Goll Mac Mórna was great and famous
he wanted a loan of them, like all the nation.

Cúrí had these shoes for a season   65
and Cúchulainn who was no mean hero;
and the once victorious Maedhbh of Cruachan
and Conall Ceárnach and Niall Glúndubh.

At Clontarf (they were there for certain)   69
Dúnlaing wore them, very contented —
if he had tied their thongs on him tightly, he would have
brought Murchadh safe from the fighting.

Sacred tree of the sunseed of Fianna Fáilbhe,   73
of the seers of Cashel kind and manly always,
is the man of great reputation
who gave to me my excellent footwear.

Though he has for some time lived under the foreigners   77
he did not learn from them to be heartless or sordid;
he has no stingy heart — indeed, he is faultless —
and it grows as he grows, the good gift from his fathers.

A generous man, and kind to the poets,   81
a virtuous man, who deserted no one;
a man of importance, a giver, bestower,
a steady and merry man and no surly boaster.

It's no false history to broadcast about him 85
that eighteen kings were in the roots he came from;
they were rulers in the land of Fáilbhe
from Cas of the light to Donnchadh the patron.

There are not many like them, my shoes, like choicest
   gems; 89
they are just right on roads of fresh blue stones;
though now sad and sore, I will soon find relief
since Ó Donnchadha chose for me these uppers and
   soles.

*Political Poems*

## The Wounds of Ireland

A sharp grief to me the woundings of Ireland,
oppressed under clouds and her people all heart-sick;
the trees that were strongest at giving them shelter,
their branches are lopped, their roots withered and
   rotten.

Though long you've been, Ireland, so genteel and
   stately,
a hospitable nurse, full of true wisdom,
you shall be, from now on, a whore to the rabble,
and all foreign robbers shall have sucked your nipples.

To crown all my sorrow, the cause of my cryings
that all kings by right on the mainland of Europe
hold their lands *in perpetuo* and they are peaceful
but Ireland's in pain — no spouse and she married!

We lost Ó Néill's root-stock, the old seed of Eoghan
and the fierce hounds, the soldiers of BrianBorú's
   kingdom;
of kind Cárrthach's blood, we have few men now living,
of Gaelic gentlemen, most powerful in combat.

It is certain 'twas the violence of injustice,
evil and spite and lies and promises broken;
no union — instead, the tearing of each other's throats
   out
that drew down on Ireland the wrath of God Almighty.

Since we lost our land (our greatest calamity),
and because of the fall of the strong and swift warriors,
through God's Divine Son and the strength of the
   Trinity
those still alive with us, may they keep flourishing.

The Gaeil lost their ways, both gentle and pleasant,    25
hospitality, charity, sweet music and manners;
wicked wild boars have subdued us severely —
I ask God's only Son to help all the Irish.

## *The Ruin that Befell the Great Families of Ireland*

*for Luke Kelly*

My pity, that Carthy's heirs are weaklings,
this poor land's people without a leader;
no man to free her, locked up and keyless,
and shieldless now in this land of chieftains.
Land with no prince of her ancient people,
land made helpless from foreigners' beatings;
land stretched out beneath the feet of treason,
land chained down — it is the death of reason.
Land lonely, tortured, broken and beaten,
land sonless, manless, wifeless, and weeping;
land lifeless, soulless, and without hearing,
land where the poor are only ill-treated.
Land without churches, massless and priestless,
land that the wolves have spitefully eaten;
land of misery and obedience
to tyrant robbers, greedy and thieving.
Land that produces nothing of sweetness,
land so sunless, so starless and so streamless;
land stripped naked, left leafless and treeless,
land stripped naked by the English bleaters.
Land in anguish — and drained of its heroes,
land for its children forever weeping;
a widow wounded, crying and keening,
humbled, degraded, and torn to pieces.
The white of her cheeks is never tearless,
and her hair falls down in rainshowers gleaming;
blood from her eyes in torrents comes streaming
and black as coal is her appearance.
Her limbs are shrunken, bound and bleeding;
around her waist is no satin weaving,
but iron from Hades blackly gleaming,

forged by henchmen who are Vulcan's demons.
Red pools are filled by her poor heart's bleeding
and dogs from Bristol lap it up greedily —
her body is being pulled to pieces
by Saxon curs with their bloody teeth full.
Her branches rotten, her forests leafless,
the frosts of Heaven have killed her streams now;
the sunlight shines on her lands but weakly,
the fog of the forge is on her peaks now.
Her quarries, her mines, are exploited freely,
the rape of her trees is pointless, greedy;
her growing plants are all scattered seawards
to foreign countries to seek for freedom.
Griffin and Hedges, the upstart keepers
of the Earl's holdings — it is painful speaking —
Blarney, where only bold wolves are sleeping,
Ráth Luirc is plundered, naked and fearful.
The Laune is taken, has lost its fierceness,
Shannon and Maine and Liffey are bleeding;
Kingly Tara lacks the seed of Niall Dubh,
No Raighleann hero is alive and breathing.
O'Doherty is gone — and his people,
and the Moores are gone, that once were heroes;
O'Flaherty is gone — and his people,
and O'Brien has joined the English cheaters.
Of the brave O'Rourke there is none speaking,
O'Donnell's fame has none to repeat it,
and all the Geraldines, they lie speechless,
and Walsh of the slender ships is needy.

Hear, oh Trinity, my poor beseeching:
take this sorrow from my broken people,
from the seed of Conn and Ír and Eibhear —
restore their lands to my broken people.

They are my tormenting sorrow,
   brave men broken by this rain,
and fat pirates in bed
   in the place of older tribes of fame,
and the tribes that have fled
   and who cared for poets' lives, defamed.
This great crime has me led
   shoeless, bare,
through cold towns crying today.

                            *(c.1720)*

## The Prophesy of Don Fírinne

Are you sad lying wolves of blackest betrayal  1
are driving our clergy into enslavement?
The son of our king, alas, is now lifeless,
buried alone and his noble son banished.

In that evil gang it's corrupt, crooked treason  5
to shove in the face of our clergy and nobles
oaths hard and false, sealed and in writing,
that the children of James have no right to his
   kingdoms.

The thunder will stop with the strength of the sunlight,  9
this fog will scatter from the offspring of Éibhear;
the Emperor will weep and flanders be conquered
and the 'Bricklayer' proud in King James's chambers.

Our land will rejoice, her fortresses merry,  13
and Gaelic pored-over in schools by the poets,
the slang of black boors will be banned and be silent;
in his bright court will James give his aid to the Irish.

That Bible of Luther's and his lying dark teaching,  17
and this crowd that is guilty and do not bow to our clergy,
will be banished across countries to Holland from Ireland
and Louis and the Prince will hold court and assembly!

# Satirical Poems

# On the Death of Murty Griffin

*a villain half-Irish, half-foreign, and a spoiler of women in County Kerry*

       Oh Death, you took Murty from us
         (and all think 'not before time!');
       take Cronin too, as you're at it —
         to part them now wouldn't be right!
Forever, rough stone, pin down with zeal
the vagrant rake who despoiled the land;
in case he pops up out of Hell again
press down on him tightly and crush his heart —
       his merciless, pitiless heart;
         a heathen who died a quick death,
       Hell hasn't pain enough for him —
         Murty so quick with the whip.
And now he is helpless and weak by the Styx
and thousands of women judge him from its banks;
under the gravestone beetles scrape his great prick,
by venomous demons and hell-hounds he's damned.
       All Hell's devils in great haste
         coloured his phiz black as coal;
       Peter slammed the door in his face,
         he went to the house of lost souls.
Since you enslaved our famous race
and turned your back on the clergy as well;
since you denied the King's son by an oath,
you reptile of evil, I'm glad you're in Hell!

Thick stone, in your pit is the thug who crossed Shannon's
   water,
the snake that collected mortgages of men who lost land and
   home;
a rotten upstart who seduced every poor man's daughter,
whose clever lips mouthed oaths against the very Pope;

a corrupt steward who craftily plundered MacCarthy's
   lands
(the fine house of the hawk from the Laune came into his
   hands).
His reward? Hell's damnation came his way
   and a bare six feet of Killarney graveyard's clay!

*(c.1712)*

## *Domhnall na Tuille's Satire on Ó Rathaille*

Vowed I'd write a satire quickly　　　　　　　　　　　1
　　for the rakish stiff-versed profligate,
for the ragged consumptive idler,
　　blind to questions of precision.

To revenge a poet flowing　　　　　　　　　　　　　　5
　　with the blood of bright Corc of Munster,
I'll hone his heart, his face, his cheekbones,
　　his lungs, the sullen clod of silence.

Baleful, rotten, unwise in judgement　　　　　　　　　9
　　(suavest when he nods and dozes);
a loafing lounger, a hungry dandy,
　　untidy, fidgety and awkward.

A line correctly the clown never completed　　　　　　13
　　(a thousand blots in its crooked coursing);
he's unable to judge things, simple or complex,
　　no taste or merit in his verslets.

Re the crown of his head: lousy and festering,　　　　17
　　black-skinned, mangy, scabby;
and nits in crowds fall down in showers
　　from his forelock bedraggled and matted.

His crooked forehead has a hundred furrows　　　　　21
　　like a miserable cat in a spancel;
and each eyebrow bulges like the twisted thorn-bushes
　　where speckled lice swarm in concealment.

The thief's eyelashes like plough-handles　　　　　　25
　　lie in his sunken eyes' cavities;
the ears of an ass like muck-shovels hang
　　all the way down to his shoulders.

Much slime and pus comes in soft gushes, 29
   mucous-smeared with fresh secretions
from the squint-pop-eyeballs of that robber,
   that lump of a dunce who's worth nothing.

His hollow eyes would make good dingles 33
   for a cuckoo about to hatch to nest in;
his grey cheeks are dull with discoloration,
   long and bent and greedy-looking.

Through his nostril-holes are seen easily 37
   his yellow jaw-bones and his gullet
with which at a feast he'd guzzle the left-overs,
   that gave a rotten smell to his liberal vomit.

His long liver tongue is like a vixen's, 41
   stretched in his back jaw and twisted;
and his stump of a tooth, yellow, maggoty,
   would lacerate crusts of bread with hunger.

          ·

A mass of scabs in his coarse windpipe, 45
   pools full of yellow pus beneath it;
this ruffian's chest's like a chunk of carrion
   torn apart by a pack of hounds in a cesspool.

This deaf fool has narrow shoulder-blades, 49
   and his hips are swarthy and skinny;
and a thousand blue veins in weak cross-hatchings
   are along the verge of his brutish belly.

      ·  ·  ·

   Shins blistered, mottled, gnarled, bandy, 62
gaunt, with hair criss-cross and bristly;
   crooked heels and thin legs of a dandy.

Dirty claws, sharp, cold and concave,  65
   huge palms with running sores that sting him;
rough and knobbly and sharp-jointed
   are his twisted arthritic fingers.

                              (c.1697)

# Ó Rathaille's Answer

I will neatly shave him and clip his nails off,
   that stooped and snout-nosed snorter;
boastful, vicious, thin and pockmarked,
   a sarcastic stumbler with soles all spotted;

from his crown with lice in droves abounding
   on putrid mange crowded and clotted
to the feet of the stiff-necked, clubfooted trotter,
   gurgling, flea-bitten and ancient.

I'll tear asunder into jagged pieces
   that fractious, raggedy, layabout;
useless and warty, a crafty hangman,
   a worm, decayed and squat and impotent.

Verminous, runny-eyed, dirty, straw-bundle,
   a rambling rover and a liar;
a skinny hunchback, a greasy gulper
   who swallows garbage down his ravenous gullet.

I will chew up the feet of the villanous coward,
   a forked thing, broken and damaged;
and his two hard heels full of chilblains
   and holes and greasy cavities.

Warped fingernails that're made of iron
   are a cover and shield for his fingers;
and two sprained shanks scalded and broken
   are peeling and chapped from singeing.

I will peck at his knees his knotted tendons
   to take away his power of walking . . .

    . . .

His belly hooped over that and hanging, 37
  a wide-groined, ruined piss-house,
a brutish paunch, greedy and greasy,
  on the lanky, bogus teacher.

A thin narrow chest, hairy and yellow, 41
  eyes of a thief that see dimly,
a puck-goat's bristles, a back that crushes him,
  rough, rotten and sallow and pigeon-chested.

A dunce and a tramp with a cord for a belt, 45
  an old burnt stalk from the sea-shore;
a hateful, tricky pimp, a sulky simpleton,
  harsh foe of the Irish nobles.

Picker at a small potato, hump in a hovel, 49
  attacker of the greasy saucepan;
a man of scabs and gaunt in rags,
  a shameless moron, an epileptic.

His throat unleashes a gust of breathing 53
  that puts in pain and sickens thousands;
from his pungent carcass comes halitosis
  through his maw and his coarse palate.

That is Domhnall, hated by his neighbours, 57
  a tramp with no strength to make up a poem;
Donncha's son, sinister, bigheaded, hollow,
  jealous and grudging, achieving nothing.

Stunted, cantankerous, with feet all withered, 61
  grotesque, guaranteed to sweat greasily;
wily, baneful, quarrelsome, poisonous —
  a cunning, senile troublemaker.

He's like a monkey that suddenly scampers
   by the side of a wall in anger
or like a rat at a run through a cloister
   with strong cats in hue and cry after.

Oh poets of Munster, a curse put him under,
   this yellow and tawny-skinned miser;
expel him, this poetical prattler,
   it's clear he wrote on me wildly.

It is not becoming for poets ever to listen
   to songs from a mouth that so roughly composes;
it's a shame for the gentry of this proud country
   to write in praise of his verses and poems.

A puny, poor creature, a dried-up appendage,
   a hungry hangman with mush stuffed in his crooked jaws,
a squatter who throws away friends for a trifle
   who chanted, unawares, against *me*, Aodhagán.

*(c.1697)*

*The Big House*

## The Poet at Castle Tochar

I have walked fair Munster's roads and streets
and from the corner of Derry to Dún na Rí;
although I was tipsy I still had some grief
   till I came to Tadhg an Dúna's.

I thought in my heart and in my brain
that the dead man dead was alive again
and caroused with the lads at meat and ale,
   wine and punch and brandy.

Meat on spits and birds from the sea,
music and singing and guzzling of beer;
spotless wax candles and tasty beef,
   hounds and dogs all barking.

The coming and going of crowds,
tellers of tales reciting aloud;
people at prayer on the cold ground
   and melting Heaven meekly.

I got a whisper from one of the rout
that 'twas Warner the bold, the merry, the stout,
who owned this famous ancient house —
   a chief not mean to strangers.

It was God who created the world entire
and gave a giver in place of the giver who died;
who for kin and poet and priest provides
   a hero, not false, but great-hearted.

# Excerpts

from *Marbhna Sheoin Hassiadh* (John Blennerhassett)

Often the learnèd came for amusement,    97
imported wine, and ales fermenting;
brandy and sugar at February's opening
and the lords of Munster merry around him.

Often the English came to visit him,    101
poets and bishops, princes and viscounts;
music in showers played lively and pleasant
in the spacious palace of this Munster Saxon.


from *Don Taoiseach Eoghan Mac Chormaic
     Riabhaigh Mhic Cárrthaigh*

Ageing authors were often in his fortress;    117
literary learnèd men, bards and druids,
poets and minstrels being served with kindness
and the clergy of Christ always calling.


from *Marbhna Dhiarmada Uí Laoghaire na Cillineac*

Alas, his houses solitary in Autumn,    165
no seers, harp-music or men of learning,
no feasting, company, wine or banquet,
no poetry-schools, musicians, clergy;

where once a crowd of joking gamblers    169
drank plentiful wine in golden beakers
and spirited dignified warriors of prowess
dancing in your father's hall to music;

with poets, priests and minstrels strolling, 173
bards and rhymers from all the provinces,
in your father's mansion beside the river Gleannúrach
(as long as my lion lies underground I will be grieving);

some of the group unexhausted by feasting, 177
repeating the jokes of all who went before us
and Gaelic stories about the wit of the heroes
of Clann Baoiscne and of Gall Mac Mórna.


from *Ar Bhás Uí Cheallachain*

I saw, she said, in his musical, royal mansion, 65
speckled silks and coverings of pure satin;
swords being honed, invalids at mead-drinking,
and the chessboard surrounded by soldiers;

quilts being warmed morning and evening, 69
feather mattresses fluffed out by young blonde women;
wines unsealed being drunk with jollity,
meat on spits and whiskey on the tables there.

Company coming to the famous house, happy; 73
companies drinking with no mischief towards neigbours;
companies proud, talking most noisily.
Perfumed aromas strongly mingling
from the tender breaths of the band of horn-players; 77
fast continuous breathing from the nostrils
of leaders who defended the battle-field;
musical tunes being played by harpists.
History being read by the wise and learnèd 81
which contains faultless accounts of our clergy
and of every family begotten in Europe.

Open doors to enclosures like amber,
wax candles lit on each wall, in each chamber;  85
casks being breached for the crowd every moment,
no stint to the flow that comes to those drinkers.
Horses bestowed on the *ollamhs* of Fódla,
shaggy steeds running together on hill-slopes,  89
mock combat of soldiers, beer in plenty
in drinking-horns of pure refined silver.
Times, in his meadow, the battle-horn sounded,
on the hills in the mist the loud cry of hunting,  93
red deer and foxes for them being started,
hares from the undergrowth, waterhens, thrushes;
in great flocks, too, the flight of the game-birds,
the royal pack of hounds and the nobles exhausted  97
on the hills in the mist after the chasing.
Humiliation to me, inescapable pain,
that meadow ruled by endless
foreign speech constantly in the gold mansion  101
which was used to the play and the rattle of chessmen.

*The Browns*

## Elegy for John Brown

The news that has eyes with tears streaming,
the reason why trees and rounded hills are humbled,
the trouble that makes great kingdoms tremble?
John Valentine's son, rots under a tombstone.

Oh Death, you lured our torchlight to you,
the hedge for our corn, our townlands, our borders;
the guard of our houses, our women, our cattle,
our protector from the flaying rabble;

our overlord, king, and shield of shelter,
our hard helmet, ever alert for combat;
our light, our guidance, our son in Winter,
our staff to threaten with, our delight, our glory;

our strong tower against foes, our valour,
our need, our sight, our greatest love, our reason;
our mien, our comfort, kind, our beauty,
our boat, our ship, our adornment, our spirit;

our Oscar, powerful, our voice, our spokesman,
our Phoenix, high, our hero, our justice;
our arms when we face superior forces,
our Caesar, strong, our star of knowledge.

Alas, the country, without you, is exhausted,
and we have no lord except the God of glory;
our woods continually destroyed by violence
and men from Leinster bellow at our doorsteps.

Magh gCoinche is solitary and spouseless,
Killarney is pitiable and tearful;
both sides of the Maine are full of foreigners,
Sliabh Luachra's in danger because of your downfall.

. . .

I am sickened by the danger facing Thomond　　　41
and new laws in Cluain cause vexation;
Grief and Gloom go announcing
that John Brown was descended from them.

. . .

It is not this weeping that so ails me　　　49
but the tears of the fair wife you had wedded;
the tears of the bright one (united so young you were)
of the blood of the Duke, his race, his relation;

the weeping of Brown, the brave, the protective,　　　53
in London under the evil control of the rabble,
his family's tears — they are all in sorrow —
and the intense and agonised tears of Mabel.

. . .

He had so many kinsmen (it's hard to count them)　　　65
of the sun-race of Éibhear, Niall and Eoghan;
there was not one of the kings of Ireland
who was doubly kin to him — no exaggeration.

And those of the foreigners who were manly —　　　69
their warriors, princes, gentry and soldiers
who did not yield to the laws of the Saxons,
their golden blood by force was scattered across the
  ocean.

. . .

The cause of wounded pride and sorry crying:
the renewal of looting and boundless evil,
the heavy increase of oppression in the province,
and the rents of your farms being counted by Asgill.

Another thing that torments the province —
Griffin and Tadhg pompous in power
by whom our great leaders all were banished
from lands which were theirs by right and justice.

Destructive ruin — your woods decaying,
Tadhg's malice burning like a black ember,
without a doubt he owns all from top to bottom
since the day the people's shield departed.

Your withering caused anguish in this country,
you, branch of the root of our great soldiers;
you were our shelter from the winds of the ocean
when the true king was banished by powerful forces.

You were gentle with the weak and feeble;
you were strong against strong usurpers;
you were not greedy, crooked, proud or devious,
but in every way a lord most excellent.

I beseech God urgently that, at your funeral,
the great Son of God and the Holy Spirit,
angels in crowds, apostles and virgins,
accompany you to the Kingdom of Glory.

*The Epitaph*

Under this slab in gloom is laid the Gaels' own Phoenix,
a Cúchulainn, a Caesar, a famous champion;

benign his face, this merry, gentle chieftain
of the liberal blood of Brown and the Pearl of Lee-side.

Oh stone, you have overwhelmed Munster's hero, 109
he's planted in earth — a cause of lament in this
   country —
the clergy's treasury, on law a sharp authority;
the fragrant binding tendril from kings descended.

Oh stone, your illwill will be forever shameful; 113
under the harrow's furrow you keep our leaders, lonely;
oh stone, your womb caused a woman ruin and torment
because John and Valentine lie prone there.

*(1706)*

## The Good Omen

Druids and prophets have unravelled,
    from previous discoveries of Patrick and Bridget
and of that true saint, holy Colm, the sayings
    which were full of the grace of the Holy Spirit;
since a prince of Cill Chais has bestowed on
    the king of Killarney his daughter,
so that place their sons would inherit
    till the world's decline and destruction.

Isaias pre-threatened the Hebrews
    that the Power that was God would deprive them
of their leader, that people in bondage,
    of their famous judge and physician;
that He'd desert them because they were eager
    in their crooked hearts to be disobedient;
if of denying of God's Son they were guilty
    He, with sharp strength, would erase them.

And thus, to us, a great God has given,
    after being so long in great straits,
a high prince, a lord and a chieftain,
    shield of strength and a new golden helmet;
that is Brown: his fame has no blemish,
    a provider, without stinting, to many;
I ask of the Man who crafted the elements
    that his princely seed shine and flourish.

*(1720)*

## *Epithalamium for Lord Kenmare*

The fish in the streams are jumping so lithely,     1
   without any struggle the eclipse is passing;
the moon's calm and clear and Phoebus is waking
   and all the birds of the province are happy.

Bee-swarms alight on fresh and green branches,     5
   there's grass and there's dew on the heath-land
since Brown has for wife our Star of Munster —
   the Duke from Kilkenny's near relation.

All weaklings grow lively, the great hills are strengthened,     9
   flowers bloom on each tree in the Winter
since Cill Chais is lovingly fettered, united,
   to the King of Killarney, our hero.

The wretchèd have relief, we've no grievance to utter     13
   about this news that is talked of by many;
this noble young pearl (God grant she's successful)
   of the noblest gold branch of Kilkenny.

The prince-chieftain's a guardian for the high and lowly     17
   and by thousands he's welcomed with cheering;
the tide's in his favour and the green wood is growing,
   the fields brighten up without blighting.

Harbours, usually under storms so longlasting,     21
   are calm, since the day of this binding;
there's a catch on the shore (not rocked by the ocean)
   of cockles and limpets and dillisk.

The Kilkenny nobles healths are happily drinking     25
   and long-life to the new loving couple;
lulling music to lyrics is struck out by harpstrings,
   most lovely and sweet is each sleep-song.

Each problem is solved, Right alone it triumphs,
    there's a new look on the faces of people;
the great sky resounds, the moon is still peaceful,
    there's no mist that blinds, no downpour or flooding.

There's beauty on boglands that can't be reddened by tilling
    from Loch Léin to the Kilkenny border;
since the noble who left us escaped his dilemma:
    long may he stay in the lands of his father.

*(1720)*

## Valentine Brown

It spread, the sore sadness, through my heart, old and
 dour,
at the coming of foreign devils to this land of ours;
the clouded western sun had rights to kingship in the
 South —
that is why I ever came to *you*, Valentine Brown.

First, Cashel without clergy, horseman or guest-house,
and Brian's battlemented mansions with black otters
 flooded round;
Duhallow with no chieftain from kings descended
 down —
that is why I ever came to *you*, Valentine Brown.

The deer has lost the noble shape with which she was
 endowed
since the foreign raven nested safe within Ross wood's
 bounds;
fish avoid the sun-lit streams where gentle currents
 sound —
that is why I ever came to *you*, Valentine Brown.

Screeching of swift birdflocks in the wind floats down
like a cat's bleak plea that in waste heather sounds;
all milk is refused to the calves by the cows
since Sir Val usurped the rights to kind MacCarthy's
 ground.

Pan, his eyes directed beyond the high lands' bounds,
wondering where Mars has gone who our deaths
 allowed;
the Three Fates' blade's revived by dwarfs and clowns
as they pulp the dead to pieces, from sole to crown.

Dairinis in the west has no free-born Earl now,
he, of the happy hawks, in Hamburg can be found;
an old grey eye weeps hard for these men of renown —
that is why I ever came to *you*, Valentine Brown.

*(1725)*

*Destitution*

## The Time He Moved beside Tonn Tóime

Long to me is this downpour night — no snore, no sleep;
no cattle, wealth, no horned cows, no sheep;
my head is vexed from the storm that blows waves wild,
and I had no use for dogfish or cockles when a child.

If the protector-king from the banks of the Laune
and the troops who shared with him — who'd pity my
   fall —
were in charge of this sheltered and inletted shore
in Duibhneach my children would not be poor anymore.

But dynamic MacCarthy who hated deceit
and MacCarthy of Lee-side are in jail without release;
and MacCarthy of Kanturk's with his children in the grave;
a grief goes through my heart: of them there is no trace.

And my heart is withered up, my humours gone awry;
the hawks who were no niggards and inherited by right,
all Cashel to Tonn Clíodhna and across to Thomond's lands
their houses and their riches are plundered by foreign
   gangs.

Oh wave down there, most famous and most loud,
from your clamoring my brain is worn out;
if help should come again to fair Ireland's shore
your raucous howl I'd stuff right down your throat.

## The Poet on His Death-bed

I will not call for help till in a narrow coffin
and, if I did, I swear 'twould not be in the offing;
whom we valued most, of the stock whose hand was
　　strongest,
his pulse is silent, his strength is gone to nothing.

My chief hope went, my brain in waves quivered —
holes in my entrails, spikes through my innards;
our land, our roofs, our trees, our fine holdings —
all pledged for a penny to a gang from Dover.

Shannon, Liffey and musical Lee are heart-scalded,
and Brick and Boyne and Bride and River Blackwater;
the narrows of Loch Derg and Tonn Tóime are turned
　　scarlet
since the crowned king's board was swept by a knavish
　　varlet.

I often groan, I am always tearful;
my fall was hard, I am unjustly treated.
No tune comes to me as I weep on the roadway
but the noise from the pig not wounded by bowmen.

The Goll of Rinn, of Kill and the Eoghanacht area
now for lack of justice is near starvation;
the hawk who possesses those lands and their rentals
shows favour to no one, not even a kinsman.

Because this race of great kings is devastated
water furrows my forehead with loud agitation;
fiercely do my tearducts pour in fountains
to the river that flows to Youghal from Kerry's mountains.

I will stop now, forever. Death comes close, does not
 delay,
since the dragons of our regions have lost their rights.
They were loved by heroes. I will follow to the grave
the lords my elders served before the death of Christ.

(c.1726)

# Acknowledgements

My greatest debt is to Reverend Patrick Dinneen and Tadhg Ó Donoghue, the editors of *Dánta Aodhagáin Uí Rathaille* (Irish Texts Society, London 1911).

My thanks to Eileen Ó Mara, formerly of Great Southern Hotels, and to the management and staff of the Great Southern Hotel, Killarney; to Siobhhán Ní Fhoghlú and Peter Denman of Maynooth College, and to the Office of Public Works.